I can see a cat.

The cat is on a mat.

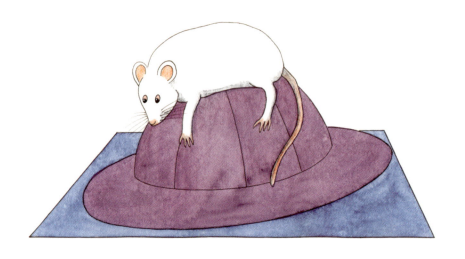

I can see a rat.

The rat is on a hat.

I can see a bat.

The bat is on the cat.

The cat jumps up and lands on the rat.
The cat and the rat are on the hat.

The cat gets off the rat.
The rat gets off the hat.

Oh no! Look at the bat.
It is coming to the rat.

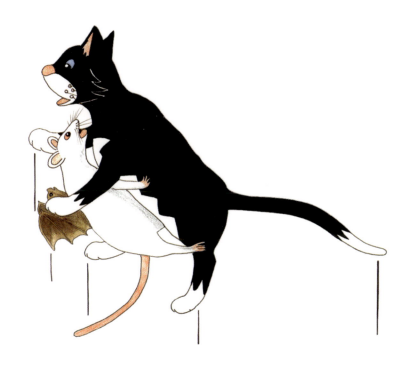

The rat jumps on the cat.
The bat jumps on the rat.

... and they all land on the hat on the mat.